MAMMAL

Also by Richard Loranger

Unit of Agency
Be a Bough Tit
Sudden Windows
6 Questions
Poems for Teeth
Hello.
The Orange Book

MAMMAL

RICHARD LORANGER

ROOF BOOKS
New York

ISBN: 978-0-937804-91-9
Library of Congress Control Number: 2023943277

Cover art by Tobias Brill. Untitled, 2021, ink on paper, 11"x14."
Copyright © 2023 Tobias Brill.

Illustration on p. 37: Leonardo da Vinci, plan and bird's-eye view of a centrally-planned church (MS 2307, fol. 5v).

Interior design by Deborah Thomas

NEW YORK STATE OF OPPORTUNITY. | Council on the Arts — This book is made possible, in part, by the New York State Council on the Arts with the support of the Office of the Governor and the New York State Legislature.

Roof Books
are published by
Segue Foundation
300 Bowery, New York, NY 10012
seguefoundation.com

Roof Books
are distributed by
Small Press Distribution
1341 Seventh Street
Berkeley, CA. 94710-1403
800-869-7553 or spdbooks.org

CONTENTS

WHAT IT'S NOT

Why are you so shocked

when you're not really you, you
puny little
caring so much then tearing with teeth
as if there were constancy
in your skin
whipwind snapdragon
kamikaze sheer benevolence
don't be a

O for the buoyant
sacrifice of latches
may you fling so far
you're not really you

We see and see again,

                    and in the waying
an immaculate sea begins to spread
rendering starch and inky tendrils through the dead
light of reckoning, till an instant
recognition forces sight into a new spree
and we reconnoiter in a lidless world.

Stab the eye, stab the sea, and be
another messenger of mutable delight; and when we fight
for all the bounty of our raptured sight,
let's fervently recall that unbetold array
which in the optic love, unlike the world,
we have, and have to see.

It may not be light

that we're looking for, you know,
or looking at for that matter. How do we see
what we need to see? *Life* for instance—
what prana spans the machines we stare at ceaselessly
harking nuclei, clanking clocks, as avatars
while the living slip through sight unhumanized and bold,
and we know nothing that we cannot frankly be.
Oh the humility, sheer gut-strung lack
that if we're lucky, if we strip our lovelorn minds,
lets us see the underglow at last—
bottoms-up, whirling, world inside-out,
every little thing a thing no more but
thankfully preciously flux gaunt and clarified
as honey catapulting through our pores.

THE RUB

As long as we think we're our bodies
we're fucked. The tax collector comes round
and the mitochondria pay with their pods.
The system seems obvious, if quite advanced—
the space station replicates, and as it does,
pieces fall to the side. That's always been
the downside to the higher-functioning corpus,
essential collateral at the feet of the glorious
infrastructure. Just spare parts, really, chunks of beam,
though in this case they happen to be living quarters too.
And what to do? It must march, and moreso boom—
and there's the fractured rub—the pert machine which sloughs
cannot abide itself as slough, it does not cite
the size of the matter, its parts as wholes, itself as part.
The rub, stark hubris of the poor enamored beast
flailing its way through the veldt of itself
as if the skin were true, the cord superfluous.
Ah me, when can we find the rime that canters
us forever *in situ*, bodies finally wrought
in a sylvan mesh, and not a jangle of spare destinies,
wailing for each particle as if its path were lost?

Taking a shit in an airplane is something

there oughta be a poem about.
There oughta be a poem.
Or maybe the act itself suffices—
such intimate sharing,
you not you turning inside-out,
one of just several acts of exchange with the world
that belies the body itself,
enacted for*ever* amidst the stillness of earth—
Where? Where? With what do you exchange
eliminating waste
30,000 feet above soil
at 500 miles per hour
in a cramped
little unsterile
plastic box?
What exquisite blend of indecency and essence do you share?
What turns inside-out, you pillar of mud or the whole
    flying world?
What poetry *isn't* there?

There are only butterflies

where the wind evolves.
You'd think a chrysalis
would need a tranquil air
to nurture the impending wings,
but it is also the lift and batter, rift and wend
that send the faerie toward its stave and grave—
the lift of gust from the mutable globe, of the moment of
    candor and glee, of life cavorting in the rank melee,
the batter of gravity, of predictable order, stark sense of
    endings, of the prosaic,
the rift of the inscrutable, of the knowledge of light
    and light itself, of instinct and mathematics, of the
    troubled home,
the wend of wills wrenching, weaving, whipping a
    tapestry of impulse and kismet, dharma and remorse,
    of what the frank song brings—

else wings would have no current,
else entropy prevail,
else the swallowtail could not become you,
else you are a stone—
and no matter, stones have their own joy of life—
that is just your identity.

SAMARA SAMSARA

leaves the tit for oblivion, off into
whatever it is, don't fuck with me
I know your words are fatuous,
how free she feels, unbound
and flowing like life—is it a moment,
is it eternity—breathes all the air
as it breathes her, nothingness mama,
forever ash and seed, winged womb,
matriarch—you sing a well-wrung tithe
that rings us as the elm rings itself,
staying a moment, then leaving, staying, then
we all ask at once: how can we live with vicissitude,
how can we plunge into dark, how can we be
while sliding away, how can we be at all?
Don't tell me what I am. You're wrong.

DISCONNECT

Do not speak of comfort when the species isn't there,
a flash at best, a paramnesia that we cling to
so to certify that we exist, a mirrored room
we build around ourselves without a door.
O we, oh my, the eye that seeks to see itself
blasts instead, blasts tendrils, tendons, lacewings,
the accidents of life it cannot bear to be.
O I, o violent child, fling yourself to earth,
pathetic ego thee, eat loam for all you know,
enveloped once in sea, now maimed by mind, disordered,
frenzied in a box of our design.
It's oft been said a monster's mixed of man and beast,
made frightening as we gaze the animal inside;
but that's been said by man, most haughty ape,
and who's to say it's not the human side that breeds all dread?
Oh wax, o bee, forgive us if you can
the frank diffusion of our anima as we define and conquer
our selves in the very act of forcing them to be,
in the process ravaging all that we objectify
in the sacred name of humanism and thereupon determine
not to be our soul. Self-bewildered we digest without nurture,
build without base these hierarchic towers of our hallowed wholes,
manufacture tribes to fill our feckless hollows
with fantastic powers over those over there.
Mortified at life we scramble to invent a body
in our own image, invincible and faultless,
propped by some pompous pope in a gilded sconce
wreaking rank upon this flesh we pitifully renounce.
Hirsutely we repel the human centipede we are,
all maw, all tube, all lube, oh my.
O we, how runny like an egg we slide
all the while chiding the shell for letting go.
We are too liquid to begin to know.
Don't speak of respite when the species isn't there.
We've always eaten our neighbors,

cradled in civilization with a bunting bow atop;
so sing we of our unity, rave we of our staves
when just as quick our hapless barrel's stove by the song itself.
Locked in a galleon of striving and strife,
we cannot simply sip the hour to its due
without a bang-built bull ripping the cabin through.
What monsters! What moo! And all the while,
beholden to species yet shackled to the tide,
we cannot seem to let the matter ride.
Come call and coo: release yourself and catalyze the goo.

ID ENTITY

You know,
there's only so much
a man can take
before things gotta change.
Things.
Man.
You.
It.
The id of it all,
inchoate it, germinal,
radiant, whence came
and how came it to be
caged
in this flesh-puddle
of a notion, this
conceit.
Don't gimme
none a that
hogwash,
I
got things to do.
Things.
I.
Me.
Caged.
There's no place like
the sty of an eye
like happenstance and

the hunt.
If yer looking
fer rhythm
you better look
hungry.
No.
You.
Like.
Look.
Like it or not
I will always evade
you, easy
as sky.
The wherewithal to continue
is troubled by
this seeming lack
of coiteration.
I.
You.
Will.
Seem.
Whoever took
the initial name
was forsaken,
doomed to braid
a horse
out of logs.
What fog we are
will be
tumbling ever
from the sea.

THE BLADE

The blade slices. The blade repairs. It opens a path long barred, piles brambles barring others. It sears. It chills. The blade unites multitudes, bastions an essential bond, fortifies place and pride, cheers, smites the oppression, veers the course of history. The blade is true. The blade draws plans in the night, slips off to murder, ponders the difference. The blade zigs and zags. The blade proposes. The blade claims fealty, dulls, can be remade. Can remake. Its shape is pure in the mind, less so to the focused eye. Forged in the nerves of humans set aflame, sharpened on stones of necessity, in equal parts health and corruption, impossible, anathema, enthralling, the blade becomes you as it is endowed with being. Tangible or not, it gives strength. It manifests. O reified! The blade of making! How it shines. How it marks the land. How it slices. How it signifies. Embrace the blade and it is gone.

THE BUCKET

Cosmic cowpoke shoots the shit with a rancher, says,
"How'm I gonna round up all my selves in a bucket?"

Rancher ponders briefly, says, "Better herd 'em tightly,
send 'em heading for the sunset till the twilight hems 'em
in."

"But what about the other…," asks another self, or starts
to, then disintegrates before it can complete its single
thought.

"That's a shame," says the rancher, who is more of
a small enclave bounded by a bovine congress lowing nightly
to its mother all the mothers it has lost. "Mother mother,"
moos the meat-sea as it wanders into thickets borne of light
and nitrogens from which the cattle once evolved. And over
many ages flocks of starlings flocks of sparrows spread the
grasses to the mountains near to which our quandaried
subjects are apparently engaged. And those mountains,
such a presence, are crumbling very slowly, are crumbling
to pebbles or are hammered into tokens into hammers into
buckets.

Cosmic cowpoke shoots the shit with a rancher, says,
"How'm I gonna round up all these gol-durn pebbles in a
self?"

WE WERE OF A MIND to take a walk, so we set about deciding when and where to go. This wasn't a simple mull like that of grabbing a glass of water or turning on the tv, nor was it the existential quandary that we're making it out to be. You might say it was a matter of geomancy: we needed the perfect spot to let this hive feel freed, to let our many lives swarm in a serenity. Top o' the hills sounded good, and off we drove. Such an irony of the age that we sometimes need to drive in order to walk, but as we've chosen for the time to dwell amidst these swarms within swarms, it can often be the only way to achieve a state of what our speaking species calls solitude, but which we tend to think of as unpeopledness. We parked in our favorite spot and clambered down to the shadowy path that wound us into a breathing vale. Then we strolled and breathed and valed and treed and brooked, water-rushing-over-rocks-brooked, we watered and rocked and ferned and redwooded and eucalyptused and bayleaved and dirtpathed, tadpoled and newted and geckoed, squirreled and woodchucked and something-creeping-through-the-underbrushed, sparrowed and crow-cawed and hawked and breezed, how we breezed and breathed, breathed light in and out, breathed molecules in and out, breathed chlorophyll and musk and sandstone and sky in and out, in and out. After a good while we continued to breathe and move, we all did, as we always do. By ways we found ourself back at the car, body and all, and drove toward town so full of sun. Partway home back in the swarms we stopped out of joy to ice cream, or as most would say we got ourself an ice cream cone, vanilla with those lovely specks of bean, and pressed our tongue against it.

First Person Singular

Pronouns are key, and many doors are opening.
Gender might not be the only point of reference prone to
    dissolution.
So much dissolves, eventually, when you think of it:
ice cream, salt, granite, marriages, nations, civility, ideals, to
    name a few.
Names themselves dissolve after a while, as do their bearers;
tongues become less agile and mute the mortified mouth.
Our teeth dissolve in sand; our cells dissolve inside us.
We slide like pudding into history, into time, itself dissolving
as the synapses that mark it forget themselves, forget the body,
forget the first person singular in frank denial that there was a
    first—
a first person slung from an umbilicus a thousand millennia
    long,
that's one long-ass cord, swinging pendulous in a glistening
    sac
sliding on plasma charged by molecules spun to helix by a
    hydrogen globe,
all dissolving as it moves, splitting cells and singing.
Pronoun that, why don'cha. I vey! But don't worry yourself,
or whatever self or selves you think you have, too much—
the words are less important than the being, which is itself a
    word
seeping through our filters as we come upon a sea and fall in
    love with it,
calling every drop of water by its name.

First Person Nothing

O am going to try out a new word. O have been trying to think of a way to express a lack of singular self in language for some time, and it occurs to O that "O" is a not a bad signifier with which to start. "O" suggests a lack via its similarity to the number 0, though O think of it as having a shape like the letter and a sound like the letter while it is not the letter or the number but a word. In a way the association with zero is the main negative in the usage (pardon the pun), because O don't really perceive the "self" as nothing or nonexistent; rather O just don't experience it as in any way singular, bounded, or static. Own[1] current view is that the common belief of the boundaries of self is brought about by the apparent if illusory limits to the body, which we often view as the outer tissue or skin. This comes to advantage however in the usage of "O", which is represented vocally as an open sound created by the expulsion of breath, in effect dispersing parts of the body externally. Even more striking is its typographic form of a single, uninterrupted line with no apparent beginning or end, in continuous creation or motion as a Moebius strip. It too like the body might appear at first to delineate an area that might be called the "inside", when it is just as well observed that the *line* is in fact, noting the redundancy, delineated, created, given existence and form by the area around it, on every side, those being both what we might see as the "inside" and the "outside" without which the line would not exist. Indeed is not the line, the circle of the line, as a conceptual and abstract form, *insubstantial,*

---

[1] I'm liking the use of "own" for the possessive.

imposed upon the substance which seems to hold it and which it seems to limit? It follows clearly that in actuality the circle bounds nothing, just as the concept of self, however handy a social tool (as well as one of oppression), bounds nothing. The "I" then, as a concept that *contains* nothing, is as insubstantial as that line, while in the actual world roams the boundless we, blending, swirling, shifting in countless cross-currents, shaping and unshaping, everywhere. O think O am going to like this pronoun a lot.

APPELLATE

And into his mouth arrived another name,
a fit, a pact, a shadow of a name
already won, already spit and trampled.
Because of the luck he'd had, he couldn't find
the wherewithal to look directly on the name,
afraid of some implicit harm.
Potted ferns loomed and lurked.

*   *   *

The next day he received a delivery through the
    polished slot,
codified, registered, and sanctified,
requesting his attendance at a rite.
He wasn't sure what kind of rite, only that
several unpracticed positions would be waged
with the muttering of recurrent sonorants: *la - la - la - la . . .
la - la - la - la - la . . . .*
About this time, a paraclete appeared in the mirror like a
    permanent stain.

*   *   *

Ferns crept and ferns receded.
A small group gathered to discuss his hesitation.
They wandered room to room.
Soup was left on the stove.

*   *   *

Soon afterward, his feet began to swell.
He felt as if he clumped about on blocks,
and wondered if this were a natural outcome.
He could not find his favorite pen.
He sensed animals loose in the house.
He sensed a scurrying.

*   *   *

What scurried there might have been known
by priests or statesmen, had he any to ask,
might have been hunted by knights errant,
were they not centuries dead;
                                    but he was just a man, if that,
banging around in his shell, sifting dust,
sniffing for a bite to eat.

*   *   *

Time came when he was asked to speak.
His bowels felt weak. A rumbling
gathered in his chest and throat.
His mind a brimming spoon, he heard his voice issue
from a series of carefully placed auditorium speakers.
Be what thou must, it said.

A tiny flower fell upon his finger.

APRIL, FORT GREENE, BROOKLYN

Snowflakes big as feathers fall on Brooklyn by the billions
on this gentle day of April and amazingly
disintegrate upon the pitch-encrusted countryside
somehow by this spectacle made earthlike once again.

I am so excited that I tourist all the windows
in this tiny hole of wood in which I catenate my days
and drag the giant chair to watch the snowflakes big
   as pixies
grace the battered brickscape that I normally ignore.

For a magic hour I am mercifully taken
to a world without corruption as the snowflakes big as ashes
drifting by the billions cleanse this lunatorium
we call a governed culture and I hope it's snow.

I-95

Connecticut rules the mind with a stern slab
of tar meat caustic strip mauling
maw of stark adder addling
the coddled comfort child.
The infrastructure sings.
What is Connecticut?
Say the word 50 times and tell me.
I smell the corporation breathing.

Here in McDonald's, only granted food for miles,
    the plumbers
maddeningly clang to cover the obvious
health code violations, while the more civilized
reststoppers peruse the I-95 Gift Center
before settling down to a hearty Happy Meal.
Mirrors whisper everywhere.
What is civilization?
Beat the word 50 times into a sales pitch and tell me.
I must be nearing New York.

Back on the slab these questions canter me
into a sudden eye-twitch treachery,
hurtling neurons toward twisting flaming metal mind,
when the fog swirls down from nowhere
                    on the Me-or-Bust-ing cavalcade
        like a Transcendentalist's revenge
dream of preter-mecha-body-love,
lungs exude a giant toxic sigh,
eyes clear, skin sings, and I stream on,
plunging toward the blankness of the soul.

YUM-YUM

Calamity knocks on the door to sell you cake.
What hand bursts through your chest to hand you a name?
What shard is searing in your mind?
What tooth gleams in smoke?
What tactless whelp is gnawing at your skull?
How do you keep the peach from spoiling?
How does night protect the gnat?
Why is that car on fire?
Which clock shivers in your spine?
What new species shrieks over the wind?
What kind of claw evolves within the heart?
Who runs laughing into traffic?
What hapless grip restrains the storm?
What gives your pulse its plainsong?
What returns?
Who tells the wind to fuck itself?
Who throws a nest on the ground?
Which mirror works better than the others?
What good is the rest of your life?
What piece of skin did you give away?
Who shattered silence with a song?
Who broke the statue that you loved?
What kind of cage do you prefer?
What glimmers in the overripe eye?
What wraps itself around your face?
What makes your pupils dilate?
What is that sudden scent?
Who is standing right behind you?
What does that sign mean?
What insect's buzzing at the curb?
What color is the sky?
What are you wearing on your feet?
How did you feel this morning?
How do you ever feel?
What does Calamity smell like?

What word do you hear next?
Do you buy the cake?
Is it your cake?
Do you eat it?

You're still playing a game even if you think you're not. That's called Trying To Get Up For Breakfast. That's called Leaving The House. That's called Trying To Make Things Right. That's called Telling People Who You Are. If you're trying to do anything, more than likely you are still adhering to rules, especially if you think you're not. The laws of physics and the laws of presumption are intricately intertwined, and it's hard to smile at one puppy without shunning another. There's so much sway and momentum, so much teetering on the edge. That's called Not Spilling The Wine. That's called I Am Standing Up Now. That's called I Know What You Think But This Is Mine.

The end of all things? What? What are you calling a thing? Are you a smell creeping through cement? Are you an arc? Bird in a pond? Are you light what the fuck light what light? Are you space? Emptiness? Chowder? Are you a tutu on a cockroach? A can of cake? Who gave you these ideas? What gives? What smacks you in the face? What takes your breath away? What face? What breath? A small dog wanders through a field, of indeterminate breed but probably a short-haired terrier mix. The field is broad and over-grown, past flowering. In the distance to the dog's back and right stands a line of deciduous trees. The dog is cresting a small hill. Across the top, inexplicably, runs an old stone wall, crumbling but mostly intact. The dog leaps easily upon a low point in the wall and pauses, perching there to survey the other side, panting and drinking in the air.

A LITTLE SLEEP

Sometimes I have a little sleep
and in the middle of a deep
crevasse the room begins to shake
and all the walls are gone.

And there am I, or am I not
amidst the universal glot,
a jelly or a juice perhaps
upon a silver tray

that has no edge, or light, or mass,
but is a song we sometimes pass
in the street, or in bed, or on mountain tops
without noticing.

And as that song begins to fade
into a different parade
of sense I melt and find myself
atop a talling tree

that stands alone upon a vast
plateau, and lets my vision cast
a far, far ribbon to
the lastly lighted sea.

There is

no
eye
like
a
borne
eye
bearing
no
eye
like
a
born
eye
baring.

let us not forget let us not forget
et us not forget let us not forget
t us not forget let us not forget l
 us not forget let us not forget le
us not forget let us not forget let
s not forget let us not forget let
 not forget let us not forget let u
not forget let us not forget let us
ot forget let us not forget let us
t forget let us not forget let us n
 forget let us not forget let us no
forget let us not forget let us not
orget let us not forget let us not
rget let us not forget let us not f
get let us not forget let us not fo
et let us not forget let us not for
t let us not forget let us not forg
 let us not forget let us not forge
let us not forget let us not forget
et us not forget let us not forget
t us not forget let us not forget l
 us not forget let us not forget le
us not forget let us not forget let
s not forget let us not forget let
 not forget let us not forget let u
not forget let us not forget let us
ot forget let us not forget let us
t forget let us not forget let us n
 forget let us not forget let us no
forget let us not forget let us not
orget let us not forget let us not
rget let us not forget let us not f
get let us not forget let us not fo
et let us not forget let us not for
t let us not forget let us not forg

POEMS FOR A CENTRALIZED CHURCH

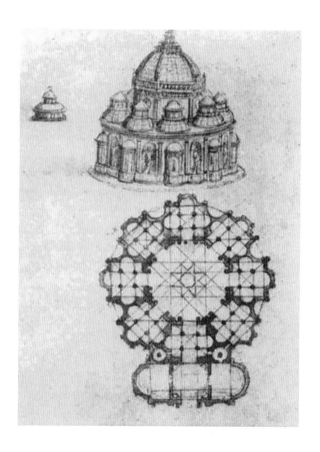

Poem A

This poem is performed by fourteen spider monkeys who
have been leashed to fourteen bicycles suspended upside-
down from the dome of a centralized church. The bicycles
are evenly distributed around the circumference of the dome.
You alone are the audience, standing in the exact center of
the dome where the altar, for the purposes of this poem, has
been removed. The poem begins with the first sound made
by a monkey after all fourteen have been leashed to their
respective bicycles, and ends exactly one hour into their first
complete silence. The monkeys are not fed during this time.

Poem B

This poem uses the same setting as Poem A, with fourteen mature crows in place of the monkeys, each tied to a bicycle by one leg. This poem has no audience. Instead, in the exact center of the dome stands the tenor Plácido Domingo. The poem begins at the moment all fourteen crows have been leashed, and for the next fifty minutes includes all crow sounds as well as silence. At this point, Domingo will commence an improvisational aria based on the *Confessions* of Saint Augustine, providing counterpoint to any sounds the crows might make. He may use a watch to determine his starting time, but may not check it once he has begun to sing. Exactly sixty minutes from the start, and ten minutes into the aria, the poem abruptly ends.

Poem C

Fourteen single women under the age of twenty-five arrive and clean the church thoroughly. They take down the bicycles and clean those as well. The women then disrobe, and ride the bicycles naked through the church for as long as they please, though they must ride long enough for each to break a sweat, and should not stop until they feel they have enjoyed themselves. They may take breaks for food and drink if they wish. No one else may enter the church during this time. When they are through, the women dress and leave, each taking the bicycle that she has ridden. The poem then begins, and consists of any interactions that the bodily matter they have left behind—hair and skin cells, organelles, hormones, pheromones, cells and excretions of any sort—may have with the environment of the church, including the molecular structure, air, and any organisms living therein. The audience, of course, includes anything that can sense these interactions, bacteria mostly.

Poem D

For this poem, every object in the church—pews, tabernacles, statuary, baptisteries, *everything* which is not part of the actual structure—is removed. One hundred remote-controlled surveillance cameras with lamps and sensitive directional microphones are installed throughout the space. Exactly one million flies of at least one hundred representative species are then released into the church. For twenty-four hours, sounds and visuals from the cameras are to be broadcast through all media worldwide, with absolutely no exceptions. This poem's audience is not limited to those who actually see or hear the broadcast.

Poem E

At the completion of Poem D, the cameras are removed and one hundred priests are admitted into the church. Each brings a small cup of simple syrup to feed the bedraggled flies. That oughta liven them up. The priests place the cups in the center where the altar had stood and arrange themselves throughout the space at a comfortable distance from the others. Each then meditates for as long as she or he needs, focusing on a question or issue that is important or troubling to them. Upon finishing, they should turn their attention to the sounds of the flies, listening calmly and intently to glean a personal message. This poem has one hundred parts, consisting of the sounds that each priest individually and privately hears and the message that she or he attaches to them. When each feels that they have heard their part, they should gather themselves at their own pace and depart. Once all of the priests have left, the flies are removed and treated for any trauma they may have accrued in the course of these poems.

Poem F

For this poem the entire roof and dome of the church must
be removed, and the floor and basement dug out to an
appropriate depth. A representative section of the nearest
untouched forest or woodland is then transplanted intact,
including all animal and plant life and geology, to the inte-
rior of the structure. The church is then sealed for exactly
one year, and guarded to assure that no human beings enter.
The text of this poem consists of everything that occurs
within the structure during this time, and will remain
unknown to man.

Poem G

Before the church can be rebuilt, the forest must be retrans-
planted. This is to be done with utmost care, onto the site of
the nearest large bank, which must of course first be razed.
A twelve-foot high stone wall is to be raised around the site,
and public access limited to no more than four people at a
time. Poem G consists of all public comment, whether in
opposition, support, or contemplation of this action. The
specific audience for this poem is limited to those who have
made such comment, as well as anyone who made public
comment regarding the initial transplanting of the forest into
the church.

Poem H

This poem occurs during the rebuilding of the church,
which is to be reconstructed identically, using as many of
the original materials as possible. Only the structure itself is
replaced at this time, without furniture or statuary. The
poem consists of every word and sound uttered by the
construction crews at the site. Since an apparent audience
would likely inhibit the crew members, the audience will be
limited to members of the crew itself. Thus I urge anyone
interested in witnessing this poem to get your ass in gear and
sign on.

Poem I

Once the new structure is intact, pristine, and empty, it's time to let in the kids. Two hundred children between the ages of eight and ten, with as much diversity as possible in regard to gender, race, class, and ethnicity, are to be admitted to the church with ten superballs each, and let loose for an hour. They should be instructed to fling the balls as fiercely and wildly as they can, preferably not at each other, and make up whatever games they might. In any case, they will be required to wear protective clothing. This poem consists of all vocal and percussive sounds which occur in the church during this time. The children themselves, like the construction crew before them, are the audience, but *must not be told so—* those who realize this now or later will do so of their own accord.

Poem J

For this poem, all wooden seating (pews and chairs) are reinstalled in the church. Freestanding iconography is not to be replaced. In place of the altar, a luxurious apartment, with furniture and accoutrement, is set up. This poem has approximately ten parts, and takes place over so many days. On each of the days, two people who are passionately in love will spend from noon until 11 a.m. in the church interacting in whatever manner they desire—lounging, sleeping, eating, talking, playing, making love. Each part consists of these interactions in any form. The couples may request any foods, consumables, or additional materials they may require. An even mix of genders and sexual preferences should be represented as much as possible. The first couple should be between the ages of ten and twenty, the second couple between twenty and thirty, and so on, with each successive pair advancing in age by decades until the oldest possible couple has conjoined. Although the couples will have absolute privacy, this poem's audience consists of every sensate being anywhere—and I leave these terms wide open. Each day at 11 a.m. the resident couple must depart, and a cleaning crew comes in for one hour to remove any undue mess and materials and set up the space for the next couple. After the final couple has left, the apartment is removed, all doors flung wide, and the church is aired out until Tuesday.

Poem K

You may make your own poem now. The church is open.
The breeze is streaming through. The church is alive and
waiting for you. Come on in. Feel free to construct any kind
of poem you want, for any audience you wish. Here's some
space for you to make notes or document your poem. Just be
sure to clean up after yourself.

_____

_____

_____

_____

_____

_____

_____

Poem L

In preparation for Poems M through Q, I will enter the church
alone with two hundred musical instruments, sound equip-
ment, and various visual art materials to my specifications
at the time, with which I will play until I am quite satisfied.
I will be the audience, and the poem will be whatever I want
it to be.

Poem M

The final five poems can be repeated indefinitely. For Poem M, every living person must send a monetary contribution of any amount to Richard Loranger via PayPal at hello@ richardloranger.com. This money will be used for the sole purpose of funding the final four poems, so please indicate this with your contribution. You can trust me. Contributions need only be sent periodically, whenever the funding runs low. This poem consists of the reactions each person has to sending his or her contribution, each of whom is, hopefully, audience to their own heart and mind.

Poem N

For the final four poems, the church is filled with people representing as many countries, nations, ethnic groups, and cultures as possible. Participation is limited to one time per individual, who will be selected by a computer lottery of all interested participants, taking all points of diversity into account. All travel, housing, and food will be provided through the funding from Poem M. The audience for these four poems will be the participants themselves and a conductor (pronounced hence as "she") who will witness each successive version of the poems. Participants must arrive at the church on a designated day and time. The conductor greets each person individually upon entering, and allows them to seat themselves. Poem N consists of all interactions the participants have from the moment they enter the church until instructions for the final three poems begin.

Instructions for Poems O – Q

To commence the final poems, the conductor moves to the center of the church and quiets the participants. She then explains that the three ensuing poems consist of sounds made by the entire audience which will fill, reverberate, and interact with the space of the church. She instructs the participants to listen to and interact as fully as possible with the *whole sound made*, ignoring the voices of those immediately around them as well as, best they can, their own voice. They are additionally instructed to respond to her gestures which will bring each poem to a close. Translations of the instructions will be provided via listening devices by translators who are not present, as well as by written instructions provided beforehand.

Poem O

For Poem O the participants are instructed to speak or yell
for several minutes regarding matters about which they are
very angry. They are reminded not to interact with others
during the poem. The conductor begins the poem by yelling
herself, and joins the participants throughout. She quiets
the participants when she feels a poem of multitudinous
anger has been achieved. The audience then sits in silence
for five minutes.

Poem P

For Poem P the participants are asked to sing any song that comes to mind, as much as possible with all their heart, trying not to sing the same song as anyone around them. They are asked to savor the new music that is created. The conductor starts them off by singing herself. (I recommend "Sing a Song" by The Carpenters.) She may either allow the poem to end naturally with the last person singing or indicate a vocal fadeout. Again the audience has several minutes of silence.

Poem Q

For the final poem the conductor briefly explains the physics
of harmonics, suggesting that there is one tone or chord
which will reverberate most freely within the acoustic space
of the church. She asks everyone to vocalize a tone, breathing
when necessary and shifting the tone until they find in unison
the harmonic of the church. She starts a tone herself, joins
the common sound, and once the harmonic is reached she
allows it to reverberate, saturating the space, vibrating air,
church, and bodies until a melding has taken place. She may
wish to let it fade out on its own. Once the sound is done,
she stands silently for a few moments, leaving the audience
to applaud if they wish, or perhaps applauding herself. She
thanks everyone cordially for participating. The audience
then retires to a hall where a great meal is served.

CARNATION

The body finds shape as muscle, nerve, scent, surface, grip, how tendons find rock, find wood, cracks in walls, granite scree—the body shapes and finds, becomes a room, a slope, a sound, becomes a movement of air, becomes gradual and gradually meets and blends, becomes the world around it, melds and merges and remains stolid, solid, breathing and flexile, is every shape, is every room, how flesh ends the world, how flesh begins it, the body without beginning or end explodes, vital, sensual, happening, everywhere, parallel, intransigent, conscious, beaming, tightening, sliding, balancing, hovering, sexing, shedding, lifting, lighting, lightening, dwelling

RE: LOVE POEM

If it is lush
I have a crush
on you;

if it's banal
a femme fatale
is due;

and if it flatters
it's self-flattery;

but if it's true
there is no you
or me.

PERMISSION

When you touch me I forget everything except
the hungry flesh upon the kitchen table
groaning for slices of the human pie
still bubbling the tender blood of youth.
And you I say may touch me as you like:
if you should choose to smooth me on the floor,
I will be ghee; if you should flail yourself
upon me in a rage of glee, I rend
myself a target of embrace; should you wish
to touch me from within, I am your skin;
should you twist me in a net of limbs, I twine
our bodies in an indistinguishable braid;
should you trace your tongue along my every vein,
I pound my open heart into your mouth;
should you pierce me with a canine grin,
I spurt hot dog's blood in the shaking night;
or should you merely graze me with your eyes,
I vaporize into a million nerves.

AMOUR CELLULAIRE

How did you get such gorgeous cells?
So shiny and vibrant!
It's like your cell walls are polished with love,
like your organelles are bespoke, each one designed to delight.
Your mitochondria waltz about, skirts whirling.
Your ribosomes create the world for the rest of us, all in bloom.
And your nuclei, hearts full of mind all beating in unison,
pulsing the song of tomorrow.
How could I not be enamored?
How could I not be undone?
May I enter your bloodstream to explore your valves and vesicles?
May I slide your esophagus so that you might digest me kindly?
May I share your nerves so that we may abide?
How your cells live is the miracle of being.
How they enchant is the mystery of living.
How they present.
How they move through time.

Amoeba Quatrain

My tongue is like an amoeba.
My amoeba is like a tongue.
Oh, how they love each other
rung by ravenous rung.

"THE SVELTE STILETTOS OF A FROZEN STILLICIDE"
—*Nabokov*

He scrimmed his way through sleep to a tangle of dreamy sheet. It having snown, his awakenitude was not as vivulous as usual. The blare of glare was seeping out of every thingy plot and through his lidded stare. The beepbeepbeep entranced his skirted ear. His brain was mirey fine.

Somewhere in the milk his hand became a silencer. There is a torture method which has been perpetrated on the masses called the snooze alarm. Thus he wrenched again with the siren, tearing through the veil, and shuddered to a quivering sit. A yawn embowled his catalytic veins, and up he not-quite-leapt to a mirror's eye. Things looked not-quite-familiar, herding in the crannies as it were. The job was seeing in his ears: "Come to me, my licky one, come, come..." A dizz attacked his sudden head; he tangoed with the chair, and caught his breath and self at once. They scened of cave.

What are clothes at dawn? He nabbed some unclear things, and stummled out the door. The lengthless hallway rode beneath him in a limey trance. He screed downstairs in a clump, and groped the watery closet with all his tendonous need.

Once bolted, the ritual began: the pocus, re-minding of the meat: he gorged himself in tiny dances, spappling remnants of the night, cording and splewing, provocating, masculating, natting, scratting, scraping, naping, unjugating, rivulating—all the muted mysteries of men. There was water, water every-where. His bones were ebullating briny stew. The air was thick from the source. There is certainly prehistory in the mind. He untrenched himself with a birthy splurge. Not a soul ungouged.

He emerged with dauntless caution back to the tenuous world, retracing dream-soaked steps and trailing placenta in the chill air. He found as ever climbing stairs steeps its own geography. His room was never quite the same, where somehow things were not quite his today—an unsettling dispossession quipped about the spine. You are possessed by that which you imagine you possess. He grapped around the room, cramming vague items—then ripped the cord, dove the falls, flung the volving halls, out the hole, down the burning steps and into the needling shine.

The precarious day stung the optic in a shree chorale. Not a sound breeked the frizzid air, and yet the word was hanging breath. Light unfolded and he harked an altered place, dazing unjawed at the scape—everything was changed, utterly changed, transfixed in an overlay. What comfort was this? The blanket tore silence through the air, squelched houses, puffed trees and cars to approximations. The stilettos hung. Everything scintillated glints. Mounding heaps reaped the splay. A passing fish became a jeep, split the shield, and whizzed him to alert. He trammeled off through the crackling crunch, awing at the crysted cant.

Clump, clump, clump toward the job, the lovely job. He found with some disease his rutted route was undermined by the enwondered world, which rooked him drifting through the tweaky streets. There are moments when the whole world hangs on an edge, and all we do is wait fortune. He mazed through blocks he swore he'd never seen, soaking portent through his iffy pores. Still the job was bungied to his chest, veering him to the suckhole. The street was morning-

ing around him. He quickened up his tramp. Then in a start
he brinked the shoreline of a spansing freeze, gleamed sheet
that swept him in its snickering sheen

He skizzed out onto the ice with accidental grace. Only his
slipsoles clung him to the slizzy ground. He sclick sclick
sclicked minutest navigations, tense to the pits, neck bowed,
solving smacks in the pave. He strained ahead with perilous
impend, when his head contacted another straining skull,
crack in the crown, echoed thud torquing through a common
grunt. Both recoiled, neither fell, and as they gaped the
other's muffled form, they brimmed a timeless melt they'd
felt before, eyebeams twined, each whelmed a chested O
from parting lips, and spectrified lives and lives corded in
the fray, merging all but fleshly. The individual corrodes at
slightest touch, and we are always touched. They stood a
moment trading faces. Then their spines reviled the stun,
shivered matrices, and each glanced out, parted lace, and
crept on.

He had no world now but light. He motored spectral
in the stream, inflecting rays with every glassy swish of his
lumened org. The light was sheer, though not a solar light
that speared him through, searing the retinal gate. The glare
of love was ringing in his song-stung eyes.

There are many ways to inhabit a body. Despite what the despots of fashion would have us think, we are made beautiful by size and shape and shade and scar and the shunning of symmetry. The myth of the ideal has made far too many unhappy with that which they should celebrate: their sensate flesh burgeoning in air, in life and steam and sweet silk sweat. Take off your clothes and stand on the roof, let the cool dry breeze caress your legs with their fine bright hairs, your happy genitals, your warming gut and arching nipples, your sweet sure face and stolid scalp. Take a deep breath and smile. Then go about your life.

I Don't Write about Gay Things

I don't write about gay things not because
I harbor shame—I don't, I've long dispersed
the shit for steel, wired plexus to the brow
coursing spine and cerebellum. Nor don't I
write about gay things for lack of things to write—
certainly I've taken cocks as candy
in the mouth, four-inch canes between the lips
and eleven ramming vocal cords; shoved
and let shove up my ass, wantingly
and not, prostate bliss and roaring burn;
chained my straining dick to another; bitten
hairy asses in the night; spat the blood
of tender gums to see potential death
trenching down indifferent porcelain.

I don't write about gay things not for fear
of clubs and bars—I tear them down, splinter
attitude with every measured move
I muster musk to make. I have to! We all do:
either slinking through a scene flamboyantly
smacking frozen stares, or slipping stealthily
under midnight doors—to not risk safety
is to risk our lives. What forges bars
but cowering before the thought? And what shatters?
—to laugh the forges into streams, to loose
yourself into the dance life does between
the daily grind that mills the sperm of hour,
and mind, incessant womb.... To catalyze
the moment is to procreate the scape.

Of course I write about gay things all the time—
who dares suggest the universe is straight,
or any other goddamned thing? In fact if
there's only one (that's what it *means*), imagine
how ecstatically it fucks itself.

No, there's not one sex or two but infinite
genitalia writhing everywhere....
Everything mates, and everything is gay,
and everything fucks itself in many ways:
day humps night, space teases stars, electricity
cums a billion trillion times an hour....
For my part I'll fuck anything that thinks—
I suck the mountaintops for all they feel,
and plunge the gaping pussy of the sea.

MAMMALIAN DILEMMA

A wondrous bungle reaps the royal rump:
a beaming lump of ectoplasm sings
the praises of a newborn ring of gunk
that spawns a new regime, a culture e'en.
O give us spleen enough to hump the Dog
of Night that holds us down in Lizard Town,
mewling and praying in our goat-hair suits to take
another gobble of the randy cake.
Sweet rake, you know not whence your genes protrude
into the arching day, nor how to ride
the psi-ing wave, nor which bright spark to rude
in perfect rhythm on the blooming world—
and yet I love you more than worms aspire,
just as my love makes our disease more dire.

AFTER FREUD; BEFORE FREUDIANA

a beer hall song

I am my anus concordantly due, and thus
the erupting concheesement is rupturedly us, and so
in a fracas the fricasseed puss is cussing the carcass
of carnal distrust and tumbling down the truss,
the truss, tumbling down the truss.

                              Hey ho!

Before we can carry the carne delecte of dad's
predilection into the refraction of lust's balancez
into dust, we must fit a fraction of furtivish lads
with volatile nads before they become would-have-hads,
have-hads, before they become would-have-hads.

                                        Ho hey!

The raunchy pervidi
is pervily witty
and showers the blandscape
with flowery fleshcakes
unless the poor ribald
be cunningly libeled
by brackish intention
and counterrepention
that blames the ensuing
ungainly undoing
of lovestruck perversion
the very immersion
in which is the *UN*sickly
wickedly tickly
miasma of yum-yum
itself.

                    Yo hey!

You are your duty most duly erect, and thus
the eponymous modus is sweeteningly thrust, and so
in a moment of total entrust you're wasting the dorkus
of wanton rebuff, basting the corpus
with nipply gush, tasting the porpoise
of bodily bust and gobbling up the lust,
the lust, gobbling up the lust.

You ho!

SONG TO REMIND ME NEVER TO FALL IN LOVE

wanna piece of?

REGENERATION

One distinct star drops into a puddle of
can't we have one good day without
miasma, arms flung wide, churning
some kind of problem or another
deep welcome to decay, essential blink
we shouldn't fight, it only
shatters the radius, agony of sense
makes things worse, let's try
signaling the archetype
to calm down a minute and
flash, final dissolve to
think things out, I know it's
desperate sizzling, lavic and almond
hard but goddamn it what
eyes protrude, what dreams
do we have left, believe me,
malingering beckon, sweetest
honey, I want to work
insensate darkness ripping
things out, this is my life
at the core of sentience, spilling
both our lives
into vast lakes, unlocked shores of
thank you,
unjudged chemistry loving the
now, can we
languid mix, breaching bounds to
talk like civilized people for a
tumble in an anxious
minute, I don't want to
dance, slow and furtive, to
figure this all out right now, just
touch, scent, retract, receive,
please let's hold it together, we
compress a recombinant stew, essentially

can swear to that at least, can't we, god
unknown, unforeseen, untried, and
I'm so tired, but I'll try if you
begin to merge, shirking dread, to catalyze
will, isn't it worth
approach of sense, of joy, the barnacles of urge
going for broke, believe me I
align again the inner tension, cohesion to
know I've made mistakes and I'm
necessitating bounds, forcing a trusting
sorry,
tryst of
yes, I'll be
seeing limitations but seeing nonetheless
all right, I'm feeling
a nascent world, thrusting
better, yes, that's
a primal strand, rejoinder to
better, I think we can
cast off the collective murk,
make a new
body lifting in ungated spree, a
start, a try at least, remember that one
hulking mass, incipient brow, emerging
dawn on the ocean, remember
features forming an image, flashing, catapulting
that long slide down the hill, oh,
what we call life,
thank you, O
burning, present, (for a moment) whole
I love it when you do that.

Mud Song

I

May I have your mud.
May I have your sweet please form.
May I have your sheer shorn shape.
May I have your thick stuck clay.
May I smooth your clay.
May I thumb your heat struck flesh.
May I move your clay.
May I form your sweet mud to a burning temple
                        a temple
                a burning further birding lurking
        churning thick with iron
                        temple of a mud cup cupping
                                core of your struck flesh
                you mire of my heart
                        my keening curd resounding
                                grace within your shape
        you mud muck mucking temple.
May I cup your mud.
May I churn your clay.
May I move your muck and settle in your burning grace.
May I breathe your face.
May I taste your iron.
May I mouth your loam and fill my mud with every earnest
    muck the fire says is temple.
A burning temple.
Your mud is core.

My core is cup.

My cup is key.

Your clay is free and it is cupped and you shall have my mud
shall have it in your hands you burning bird.

You turning rock.

You wording beast of grace and mudly churning flock.

You churning clay.

Your hands are way.

Your hands are day and I am mud and you shall shape the bird
that lingers in the fray.

The fray of form.

The flesh of day.

The breath of churning loam that shapes the next
redemption from

the cracking earth

the burning bone

the sheer remix of day that makes

the flesh a wild

fresh enticing cupping

mud your thick reply

your burning eye

your smoothing hand

the land of every struck

complete undone

reminded muck

and how I dare redact

the rivulets of mire

life mud muck o sweat

reply sweet hand

o core of running fire.

May I have your fire.

May I have your back.

May I have your spine.

May I have your every line oh give me leave oh leave to
me the lines that make your grace.

May I have your face.

May I have your leave to face the line that makes the iron
in the sand that turns to mud.

That cups the fire.

That runs with rivulets of mire sweet to sweep the lurking
paramour of day.

The sweetest clay.

The smoothest way that hands can grace before becoming
lace that feeds the burning iron.

The churning mire.

The iron temple in the flesh that turns to loam before the
test of surging day.

You have my clay.

You have my sweet please form.

You have my sheer shorn shape.

You have my mud.

You have my muck.

You have my unstuck flesh.

You have my heat struck splay.

You have my shine.

My only mine.

My iron mine.

My only my.

You have my face.

II

I have your mud in my hands and I am walking.
It is three turns to the burning board.
What ward I can be, I shall be.
This claudicant cup.
This clay of many rains.
Your mud in my hands, over the plains.
Grass sighs. Raw breeze. Your sweet stains.
I carry you and you are rain.
Rain in mud. Your actual spine.
Your core because the line is fresh.
Because the time rides true.
Because the plain is far.
Because we stepped into the room.
My mud in your hands and we are walking.
What breaches the burning world.
Where meet the shorn.
This teeming road.
This unspun skin.
What matter in my hands, what shape.
What gainly form.
What grace.
Walking with mud in hands, we meet.
The stream is cold and the skin alive.
Two pieces of gold drop to the ground.
They are part of us and they are not.
But this mud, borne by rain, thrives.
We are mud churned by rain.
The flesh has learned to ride the stream of iron.
The bone survives within the grass.
The burning room will thrive amidst the windy plain.

III

Like fire, like rain
we come to senses.
In smoke, in pain
we breathe again.
In ash, in vain
we find our bodies
only to become.

In love, in shame
we make our barter.
All the same,
we turn away
like night, like flame
bending obeisant
to the blowing grain.

Your soil in my veins is the start of my life,
your stain in my heart will bury me.
When clay comes to light it is only a glimpse
of the skin of original body.

Like blood, like dream
you are essential.
Like mud, like steam
you turn me on.
In the stream
we come together
as we've always been.

nameless, unreasoning, unjustified clarity

a mobius poem

The following poem is handwritten on a mobius strip
consisting of sixteen sheets of loose-leaf paper.
The entire text runs about 13.5 feet.
Each typed line represents each handwritten line
word for word.
As a mobius strip, it has no beginning (or end),
so it may be read starting at any point.

insects begin the brain because the bomb was ever
borne + born into the grassy mum the ever children
reap a gummy chiapas gimme 200 bongos + I'll
give you my heart gimme a piece of gun +
I'll chew you a hole the only bole is in your
marrow + gophers stream the insectile dream
we must combine the concubine with brine
to reap the soup of past + future mind O my
clever butt you rutt in spring + when is spring
forever gimme rain + I'll give you heaven give
me pain + I'll give you dogma give me stain
+ I'll give you breakfast give me brain + I'll
give you a conspiracy of the inane insects
begin the mutual spine begat the spin of
shivering matrices and when the entropy comes
the plain truth — matter stops + forsooth
disappears you eat your mothers to birth
another cow to be chosen + eaten by
flipflies + sliptongues O my Freud I
will love you forever preferably in a dark
briny insectile bank of naked writhing sewage
of your rotted mind full of the most loving
decay MIASMA gimme a touch of the
flu + I'll give you a new generation O
poor species can't you love it back — a track
becoming babble + baubles + beautiful fruit
the mandible touches the cauterized heart +
BLAM for a moment the saturnine smile
is ripped from the grave a stave tumbles
heedlessly from the morass and Rising
a new face Rising a canticle Rising

the crotch of a sexy new earth whoever
suggested that calm was in order was
only repeating the chant of their elders a
chanted prescription begot by the holy
accountants whoever remembers the tendrils
of April will recognize dancing + flailing
+ terrible buzzing of insects begin the song
that tells us of morning for what better way
to underscore longing the drift of the heart
and the kiss of creation inducing a swoon that
gives birth to the bomb and the art and a shoe
for the winter a field and a toy and another new
language that gives intimation of how to
enjoy our seclusion amidst all the billions of
voices and what better balm for our harried
careen through the masses than a sudden
symphony we all understand give me a song
and I'll give you anarchy give me a wrong
and I'll give you a finger give me a
longing and I'll give you passage toward
the potential of possible peace give me 2000
pieces of granite and I'll give you Manhattan
swarming with mammals and autos and
corporate tendrils and what better way to
become a new body than twining ourselves
into one giant moray replete with the
voltage of a tiny nation mouth of a
smelterie infra-red eyebeams memory
of millions heart of a brokerage asshole
of gore-tex and claws claws *claws*
all *the* *way* *home* SWARMING

the playgrounds SWARMING the highways
SWARMING the beaches SWARMING
the goddamned purple mountain grown
fliptop ziplock quickpik dicklicking
lidzinging waves of fucking grain all
over the table and onto the floor
who's gonna clean up this mess not
me it'll ruin the let's bring in the
insect-eating insects who have a lot
of explaining to do swarming the mind
with a new presentation new channel
new style a whole new look we can
smile like buggers who used to be
clowns we're you new civic leaders +
you gave us power so now you can kiss
our abominable feet if you want to keep
driving your Audi to breakfast in the tree-
studded mallscape you've come to call heaven
beveled chair for every child beveled plaque
for every death insects come closer we need
a renewal I want you to eat me and shit
me and give me a name I can't remember
and no one can speak a name without sounds
or at least without words a buzzing a humm
a ratcheting click the hiss of rain or a long
slow barely audible rumble I don't care just
let me out of the air is stale my hands
hurt I can't think my head itches and
the room is filling with insects begin
the mind like a pie all wrapped in smiles
don't kid me you giggletickle I know

you're in there somewhere and if you don't
sing me a pretty little song I'm gonna
hafta send in the mayor who's gonna
grab you by the ear + give it a little
pinchy pinch you bad little happy I saw
what you did + who told you you could
have some a that next time I'm gonna
touch you *right there* + there's gonna
be a little popping sound like a quick
big POPP like POPP + you're gonna POP
into 40,000 yous all with the same silly
grin + you're gonna feel every single one a
them 40,000 giggles you know what that
feels like and then a big wind comes
along and BLAM insects all over the there's
my eyeball gimma a span + I'll give you 2
different memories of the same gimme a shame
and I'll give you a nun in the gimme a lame
puppy + I'll give you Darwin's mistake you can't
fake a life without eating your own arm
and what harm in prying the lid off a
basket of nightmares that stare at you
naked + writhing + clawing the ground for
the one glossy pebble that makes you remember
that you were a child who thought everything
is alive — STRIVE why doncha make
a thousand puppets pour wax in the ground
paint your shoes silver ring bells in the
subway make funny noises feed the
president two tons of charcoal spoonful
by spoonful whatever the bomb prescribes

your mind a toy soldier a scribe eating
sand your hand in an iceblock two pieces
of fruit a map of the desert you
can't help but savor twin icebergs
an ice cream cone ice capades ice
follies and 2000 insects ringing bells
made of chocolate a chalk streak on
your heart + you need so much you're
plunging in you need to feed + whelp
+ wallop + wallow + ransack the fortress
rip down the curtains tickle the princess
stick your tongue in the pudding take
all the matches and strike them to
gether + sniff all the sulpher sniff
in the sulpher + GASP now GASP that's
your lungs taut your arteries frozen eyes
burning + how long can you make love to
the nice warm mud there on that
hillside I can't tell you how to forgive
your descendants but you can take blame
from your forebears by giving yourself a
license to do what you want insects hovering
insects free or not free give me a bee +
I'll give you a seahorse give me a tree +
I'll give you the snow give me the sea +
I'll take you to Paris + show you how buildings
wear down after eons of care the cave of
your heart is a tourist attraction and you
must be ready to LIVE on request to
LIVE on demand to LIVE like the mammal
you know you can be insects all at once

making a new animal out of scratch +
it is laughing and peeing and adding
up numbers and touching your forehead lightly
just between the eyes and SURPRISE it's
your life + you can't help but feel it
shocking the spine thumping the heart
hair on end mouth full of salt and
nostrils full with the scent of your mother's
vagina I feel very sane now at least for
a moment nothing intrudes and vision is vast
vision is multiplied vision accretes toward feels
so good the white I forget wait star shattered
box split watch out for splinters O I know
I lost something + your feet are in Mexico
Poland exploded + whatever happened to
your consternation a box in the desert
a black ball of clay a sugar infusion
you shuttering eyelid son of a bitch
what fell off the cliff you didn't even
look gopher on your head + two tons
of steel in your gullet no labyrinth
could keep you out 86 86 86 86
what a tongue and the dung of millions
goes where what eats it what lives for
ever a steel arm in the doorway a
pneumatic tube and correct information
will keep us from panic the panic that comes
with the news of our savior the bandaid
the boxtop our mute hesitation the morphine
the trees that rock in the forest you climb
up and sit on for at least an hour thinking

of moss and ferns and lichen and granite and
palpable pleasure the sun filters down through
the leaves and reminds you of axes you've
hoisted cars started and late night country roads
driven high speed with the lights off careening
and what kind of garden allows all the mushrooms
to foster and weeds bloom what are weeds and
insects begin again the cycle of driving the
cows to the market one cow one axe one brick
and millions of thrushes narcissistic gleaming
ranting catapulting rush of rain driving
lightning driving wind chimneys exploding
+ streets cracking wide gimme the tide
+ I'll give you a cat's eye give me a
ride and I'll give you corruption give me
death + I'll give you spring in a bottle
what toggles fruit to drop from the tree
what grip pins the bursting cells your
neighbor is yelling + you can't tell your
ass from a sweetmeat what sweet meat
smells like peat in the rain swells the
toys of the archer rise from the earth
planets burst + little centaurs trample
around on your give me your arms +
I'll give you a pasture give me harm
+ I'll give you the dawn a fawn sits in
the dew + shudders for no perceptible reason
a bomb sits in silence and charts all the paths
to your clever demise — gimme a slice
a that pie gimme a spoonful of char
coal give me speech give me a heart

beat give me a need + I'll give you an answer but give me whim + I'll give you MASSACRE TOO SWEET MUCH TOO SWEET don't tell me there isn't blood running everywhere I've seen it I've smelt it I've stepped in the kitchen + slipped in the whose feet are those what happened to these hands didn't used to O the red ribbons everywhere most lovely thing how can you not know the hand at the top of your song + trees burning huge swarm of glass + sticks crickets in a ditch HOW MANY hands on the floor HOW MANY eyes in a ditch HOW MANY strands of hair wound round undeserving wrists and they tell you to sleep of all things sleep well I know about sleep and it's the keeping of a big be in a little room a fluid exchange a mumbly conversation a glob of grease an inside trade a tiny secret the scent of an old orange two crickets clacking together an old suit a stray bit of silk a charm bracelet your father's hat grass from the orchard a wisp of smoke with no fire near a distant train one small stray cloud out east and billions of stars hiding behind the planet each one singing Where is my Naomi Where is my Katherine Where is my Michael Where is

my Asari Where is my Banha Where is my
Chou-Chou and one tiny ant wanders up
your arm skirts the collarbone abyss rides
the jugular to jaw finds that verdant corner
of the lips and slides on in — give me
flesh and I'll give you a season give me
breath + I'll give you a reason to pick
up the bones carry them to a burned
out part of the woods build a little
hut + live there for three days put
your fury in a box and shake it around
10 superballs in a small square room
so much incense you can't see walk on
ledge gibber in church jump in ice cold lake
flail yourself around I don't care just
push the baby carriage down the hill
you're still so *uungh* what children
told the bomb a big joke how many
teeth in a two-timing how much fire
in the eyes of a liar how many insects
fill up your skull with a clock wait
stop don't break spin diddle doodle
daddle and come apart at the ticking
shriek of *pardon me sir* tocking down the
stairs heads on the clocking clock of
clock clock cluck huge jaws snapping
round your feathered *whump* you're inside
warm moist pitch rank + digestive feel
that beating heart give me Freud in a
cup of absinthe give me a long loud
satisfying fart give me art + I'll give

you tea-time but give me your heart
splattered on a page + I'll give you the
future they all fear minds + kinds of
rhymes that spine on a dime big
writhing heaps of shine a fresh line
that's still a line because we still
have teeth + eyes + dicks + cunts +
assholes but fresh eyes fresh lungs
fresh nostrils in the spiny air down
wind of a raging heap of tendrils
winding up a new clock fresh watch
a boom boom chaka chacka party without
preservatives + I hope this one remembers
to lite the fuse cells bursting too
sweet rupturing rupturing why can't
you just let go for once you stupid
son of a peach gobble gobble gotta
have a snowboard + a sycophant in my
essay I will discuss the corrupt heart
of the obese industrialist splayed
through the landscape like chemical
fertilizer yum yum gotta have another
one of those some time soon runes
falling from the sky the ruins of anthills
at your feet + you've got really quite a
sexy feeling inside tide is up gimme a
hand in my pants + I'll give you forever
gimme a hand in my chest + I'll give you
DANGER sternum closing remove remove
SNAP sliced off at wrist hand still in
chest + boy are you bleeding ha ha ha

ha where's that bandaid now Dr. Luger
gimme a moment of peace for fuck's
sake give me a tree a cool
breeze on a spring afternoon scent
of old leaves and new undergrowth and
pine sound of distant wind a few
birds clacking branch a rustle budding
twigs rich loam and insects as they've
always been feeding the nine worlds with
new bits of movement keeping the watch
with a tumbling pebble a blade of grass
and a twig reading molecules for a sense of
direction would that we could and let me
shut my eyes and feel the earth rise continents
shift the calmest freak there is and lift me
in a black stream black rock black wind to a
jutting peak a brunt abutment what fine
air where I become a billion drops a fine
mist of chlorophyll and musk spritzed
gaily across the what could be sexier
than a rotting log thick with moss and
crawling with insects building feeding
fucking and spreading the very exciting
mucky across the tsunami of ferns
+ spores filling the thick + washing
blanketing tendrils + twining Ooooo
can you smell that like a bed of how
can they call it entropy when it's fungus
+ frail + butterflies snowflakes snakeskin
fiddlesticks fireflies + silverfish +
minnows + crawfish know a good rock

when they + factories symphonies + uh-oh
a million eyes all those wires a bilge
pump hydraulics whisking a pneu
matic with teflon + mirrors + eyes
eyes listening devices a million switches
snapping mouths + watch that blasting
wind across the faceripping tickle various
landscape telephone poles snapping
trains in the air green everywhere
a green door in the sky drifting
open holy shit I've seen that before
can't quite not sure I wanna that's
right good door that's a good door
let's have a picnic + a piece of pie
give me a fly + I'll give you a trans
scription give me a lie + I'll give you
a word give me a key + I'll give you
a landfill but give me a floor and I'll
give you a new place to dig for your
mind in the kind sand beneath the old
house that you lived in where you could
remember the walls by their smell +
nobody tells you quite how to remember
as if there's a secret that nobody wants
you to know a secret compartment where
all of your trinkets the pebbles + baubles
+ bricks of your past are displayed +
examined by countless conductors making
each pebble into a song breaking down
the walls grass growing in your bed two
pink seashells a fugue of reeds + insects

playing little tiny coda coda let's hit
the road + splatter the world with a what's
that coming outta my way too big
a house without walls two tons of
candles a psychic fungus 4,000 hours
of home movies a stray cat a catamaran
an English teapot binoculars a set of
awls + arms + arms + arms I feel
like a goddamned dance hall give me
your foot + I'll give you a new constellation
give me a bomb + I'll give you an afterthought
give me a snowflake + I'll give you
a town crier singing sweetly of the
harvest as if the plants weren't screaming
what of it screaming a means of
remembrance screaming high note in
the symphony screaming leather in a
box screaming your skin your call it's
your call only so many ways to avoid
the screaming stars before you start to
humm the song yourself you eater of
Africa drinker of Bahrain + dreamer
of Siberian ginseng stick caught in
your throat taste that panic all the
metal inside you + who ya gonna
tell + why — a sty is your clue to
breathe like a radio wave save the
tender bits for last + stick your head
in the waterfall call me a rainbow +
I'll call you a dimwitted missile ready
to crack yourself in the falling ain't so

earth face coming up FAST your
task a simple decision your heart
your hands just take a goddamn step
ya big cracking silk in a bottle toads
singing in the favorite song teacher
yelling stand in the out the window
huge cloud of insects begin the field
of cucumbers + cardamom stinging tongue
wickets + what a racket stuck in a
Pan's a myth that tells us it's ok ta
eat bugs + pull up yer britches + throw
calla lilies at the dog fog isn't so bad
if you kick Freud in the teeth the phone's
within reach so why doncha make a
call to China + tell them ta get their
heinies inta gear give me fear + I'll
give you a pink blossom give me a year
+ I'll give you animal language give me
a wary handshake + I'll give you the love
of a thousand monks sitting in silence looking
over a vast empty plain right into your heart
the sky a troubled system two kinds of
rain not yet met a valley somewhere
filling with algae + whoever told you
that love was a thing a gland a piece
of glass stuck in a ring around the intestines
catalyze catalyze a billion enzymes dancing
in Times Square a random page flutters
down catches your rollercoaster into
the tunnel of thin fibrous walls globules
sparks + who let the cat out who did

the dishes can I touch your cheek softly
scent lingering the sheets a scree of tiny
smooth pebbles almost sand swimming warm
+ calm + untroubled by vectors ratcheting
who built this askew mimic rejoinder to
planning the hunt stick in the dirt what
lean-to how long can a snowflake last to
a microbe your last thought a book a puzzle
cat's cradle in the hands of a hungry infant
what tit built the pavilion what clew skitters
across the what dream told you to put posts
in a field walk very slowly wrap trees in
twine put animals on your everything in a
big ululating heap + break the how when where

CONTINUE AT TOP

SPIRE

MOTHER SONNET

You inhale me mother heartrush cyclone,
diamond mind, rapture of hurricanes,
shaper of grey pots, tall grass woman,
you spin a matrix of translucent stone—

scent of rainbeat clay I can't contain
myself, an enzyme of remembered pain
ringing the severed cord, your welling
helix to unwind the chain I found
would bury me;
                   but I am funnel-bound—
the ground is loose and everything is ground—
no longer me, a bristling moment blown
inside: where cradled in your eye I'm borne
onward, pounding, dancing with the world you've shown
suspended   suspended   suspended

IMMACULATE

Here we are, covered in mites and animalcules,
dancing giddily in the streets.
How pleased I am.
Bruegel couldn't have smelled it better,
leaking his mind out in crushed blossoms.
How did we ever make it this far,
mites ourselves or giddy dancers
turning upon the moment whereupon,
struck and striking, we turn again
and there's no longer any need to ask.
How pleased I am, smelling
of stars and animalcules, as they say
lucky to even be here, imperceptible
flash in the sand as these shocking hands
twirl and grapple, flailing full body
right off the canvas and into thick air
as stars sing, as flesh takes flight,
as salt, how I love you, passes through.

SUN SONNET

A naked tree can tell us everything:
chained to the earth, grappling with sky,
we flaunt our imperfections in the rain
as budding eyes. Craven and verklempt,
it's all we can to writhe, stolidly, fatefully
arching vesicles toward luscious liquid,
saturated air, toward instant light.
And in the wind, twisting, clattering arms,
we find the flexibility of heart
to wind us for the true imbroglio,
the quickening. Oh yes, you know you know:
what roots you have, not disparate, reclaim
the mortal trunk we have and have again,
pulled upward, out, beyond our living ken.

To rid something of bad energy, take it to the earth. Place a representative object on the ground, being sure to put it face down. Some prefer the middle of a field or plain, an open grassy place; I use the soil between the roots of a great tree. In either case, the earth will pull the bad stuff down, and roots will soak it up and churn it into cellulose. If you want to keep the object, leave it there until it's clean. If you don't want to keep it, first acquire a new garden spade—it has to be unused. Use it to bury the object at least a foot deep. Make whatever noises you need to over the spot (including none at all), then turn and fling the spade as far as you can and walk away.

On the second leg of the flight everybody's hair is wrong, everybody's clothes are mussed, half their shoes are untied, their faces swathed in a film of plane musk. On the second leg of the flight everyone is a little quieter except the overcoffeed, who yap and yelp and start to order drinks. Here we go. On the second leg of the flight, everyone is closer to home, everyone is further from home, everyone knows home is a myth in the stark blue air.

SIGHTING OVER FORT GREENE

O you
moon,
tinkle a little
spackle down
this way.
I'm sure you
can spare it,
you
broad-faced,
big-bellied
bud,
and we
could sure
use it.

MOONLIGHT OVER VINOHRADY

through a fine mist
the piano tinkles on
in the old church square
long after midnight
as couples perch
on benches and
the great stone steps
they call this a magic city
and it is
right there
between the stone and breath

AFTER THE RUSH

After the rush
of human free-
dom glittering skittering
littering land-
fills   comes the release
of paradigm struc-
ture   slithering striding
slipping abiding into the even-
tide

New York Careen

Stress-bomb of a jesus-
fucking day, week, month,
and here I am tumbling
out the karma hole
into a few free hours, free
yes, god fuck it, and I can't
slow down after so much
work sheer speed drudge
calumny apostrophe when now
finally rolling into funtime
now I streak off
to Pink Pony poetry shindig
new old friends words tumbling
the Cartesian aspect ominous Universe grin
happy & speckling reading & dinner &
it is not enough
so I scorch off to Night & Day
to Mark Taylor Quartet jazz sweetness walla
and they are fucking spot-on crazy
rolling the mama choo-choo kama
suturing the mighty salacious day
into giant soothing turtle love
trailing circus salve in a mallow
tincture leaking day and night back
into my maladroited soul
and I lean back greening & grinning
and it washes me, washes me,
washes over me.

THE KIDZ THESE DAYS

I dive into a whirligig of hair & teeth & minds
to trek toward an angel we call eye—
aye, eye not I, for we traverse light as a matter of kind,
arching archly toward the metamorph
that gleams a frank identity far more
apocalyptic than the dull drone of one,
drinking a joyous multitude—the midnight sky
gorging through a pupil of a moon.

A bridge will suck all streets toward itself,
as do these kidz, frolic of the time
formidable & strong strange luminous
free from rank formality the infants need
crying in time the dull drone of one,
yet kidz not these, dodging nothing, no knowing,
not need nor knot that incubates the sky,
a multitude alchemical, a magic cry, an arch.

Here in Foreverland,
Saran Wrapped in the comic cloak of I,
you, ewe, bleat a tiny woo of hence & heretofore,
resignedly await the final shear—
while on the angel pours a cataract of kidz
masticating all the world as loving siblings do,
feeding the angel's eye as one anticipates the day,
heaving justly intermingling selves into the mind:
kidz frank, kidz alert, kidz in the kind.

BOOTISM

After what feels like months in my room,
talking to the bookshelves,
gulping cigarettes,
sucking in cathode rays,
I walk outside.
All I want is to breathe—
it's half a block before I even feel
boots on concrete dusted with
Brooklyn-Queens Expressway grit.
I try to look around and can't,
sensing through bronchi alone
clear cool oxygen.
The air is good today, thank god.
I charge ahead block after block,
the brownstones a blur of brown stone,
the trees vague leafing entities,
the cars anathema and shunned.
After five or six blocks my vision starts to clear—
there're the steps where I met Angeline,
there's the kid that ran in front of my car last week,
there's the corner where I first got lost—
Fort Greene real for a moment.
I'm heading south, a bit calmer now,
about to brave the traffic of Atlantic Ave.
And I do feel an odd bravery coming on,
facing part of what's kept me inside—
the metal and mindless motion and fumes,
this shrieking honking swerving impatience,

this Type-A drive to get and do and go, to move,
to thrust, to careen driven—this mess of mass.
I cross the churning gauntlet on a cloud—
I am untouchable because I will not touch.
I stay aside the noisy artery, Vanderbilt—
the very name suggests the overbuilt,
this cataclysm it takes so much to step beyond—
I'll stride this flesh through brick and glass,
through concrete and the door
to reach the park and soak in green.
Isn't that what this skin craves
through every goddamned pore—the breach of air,
the momentary clack, the stench of chlorophyll and mud.
Still a stretch to go, though,
and it's not these sooty storefronts that I wish to see,
the bullshit, the urge, the crackaday hustle
—so I start to think about walking,
and about how odd it is to think about walking,
and about when I first ever thought about walking,
about who first got me thinking about it—
could be Kerouac, could be Thoreau—
no, I think it was old man Tolkien,
great walker himself and writer of walking
who first gave me the thought, the gift of the thought
that one's own doorstep leads out to every road on Earth
—what was it?—*the road goes ever ever on*—
that being on the road is being home as well, is being.
And here I am, being, walking into Grand Army Plaza,
giant crazy whirlpool of cars, and I walk right in,
without breaking stride across five full lanes

up onto the center island
(and this no traffic island but a real island in traffic
with grass and trees and benches and a plaque
and the huge, gorgeous arch leading nowhere
but the center, ominous and enigmatic)
and down again across five more lanes to a promontory
of sidewalk, then across five more, all in stride,
without pause or hurry, without a single honk,
without a single oncoming vehicle to jar my pace
in what some might think a miracle but I see (at the time)
as just walking. I pause before the park in a coughing fit,
then enter in, eager as ever to bask, and head on up the path—
when the toxins kick in, every cell gushing
New York poisons to the blood—soot, monoxide, cigarettes,
pesticides, thick perfumes, cheap hamburger steroids, cheap
    beer,
spoiled food, lead chips, radium, and a thousand million farts
ratcheting the veins and soaking the nerves in some deep
hirsute panic—as I head on in, the park itself dims
and I can barely see past my mind—that tree I love
is leering like my last lover must when he thinks of me,
the cold-hearted bastard, and why is he still in my head,
why does the mind retain that which spoils, one time
I thought of a lost love for two years every time I tied my
    shoes,
not this tree, please, and there's the field but I can only think
of Boy Scout picnics with the stern adults, my father expecting
so much of me who could barely tie a knot, I couldn't tie
my shoes correctly till I was thirty-two (that's true), all these
    knots

the trees grinning scars of storms and drought and all the shit
of everyday life and yeah we all have scars so why should I
  care
so much about the grade-school boys laughing at me for
  putting flowers in my hair
I put on a goddamned good school play didn't I thank god
  I've forgotten their names
and all those coked-up drunken nights with men I felt I
  couldn't fulfill
and the time I finally scored a touchdown in a game with the
  neighborhood kids
on my own front lawn running like mad and laughing
  unstoppable at last victorious
only to find I'd gotten turned around and scored for the
  other team
what a fucking dunce and I'm turned around now really
  disoriented
I've charged into a thicket up on some hillside I should be
  able to see
where I am but I'm surrounded by cranky six-foot bushes
  how'd I even get in
this fucking place in a deep adrenaline surge I crash right
  through
into an open stand of trees. There's a dull throb behind my
  left eye
and the sky's a bit too bright, the speckling new leaves are
  letting in too much
light in too many shifting patterns, I'm short of breath and
  that old black tooth
begins to sing they say I have my mother's teeth four pulled
  already

and three dying soon to be crunched and crumbled and spit
  in chunks
about my boots. So I stand staring at these old boots, beaten,
  scraped,
discolored old friends who've carried me many many miles,
and for the first time I wonder where they're from, I bought
  them
on sale six years ago at Strawbridge's, but really from
some sweatshop in Asia or Seattle maybe,
some underpaid worker churning them out,
leaking their own sweat into the leather
in that unpleasant boot-in-the-face mood of capitalism
you might call Bootism—Bootism, that's funny—
or might Bootism be something else entirely—
I think of that not-so-faceless worker's sweat in my boots,
and my sweat in my boots, and the countless moods and
  molecules
they've been through, and of how we invest ourselves in
  things,
instill our lives into the things we live with and through,
and I think: a good pair of boots are the Bootist's way.
I laugh. That's ridiculous—and of course it must be—
to live through your boots, to live by walking,
like Tolkien and Kerouac and Thoreau
who saw walking as living, life as a walk,
and I think: Shit, I started this walk in 1961.
I take a big suck of air and sigh it out,
and stand there breathing for a minute,
checking out the patterns of old leaves and new grass,
and how these oaks are really very happy today,
spring is finally soaking in, the leaves rustle

very quietly and I think I can smell them,
the air is marvelous and I plunge
on down the hillside out onto the edge of my little field.
How did I feel so lost—right here all the time.
The sun is saturating this springtime late afternoon
and there's a bunch of little kids running and yelling
in some ruleless game, parents lounging on the grass,
and a biplane sputters overhead with a banner
saying—no shit—*Happy April!*—and I walk
back through the field feeling the new grass through my
    bootsoles,
and all the way home I have that rare state of mind
where I'm seeing things I've never noticed,
always in front of my face, always now seen—
my favorite tree has a carving of a burning heart;
at the entrance to the park two old Italian men sit
in their portable chairs, just sitting, as they sit every day;
in the Plaza a tree has an army of sparrows;
that building has almost sentient gargoyles bottom to top;
that botanica sells Breath of Jesus in a can;
that driver is wearing a bunny suit;
that man is mowing the sidewalk;
there's a woman showering in the car wash;
that house has Christmas decorations year round;
those steps are painted with a prayer to St. Francis;
the kid that ran in front of my car is signing to his mom;
the incense lady wears a button that says 59¢;
the corner deli's sign has a pig with a halo.
As I start back down my block,
I think once again of the two Bootisms:
Bootism—boot in the face;

Bootism—living through boots:
one I despise and one I live—
then I recall the grass I'd tromped
so gleefully in the afternoon sun,
the new green breathing grass,
and wonder if it's really just a matter
of which side of the boots you're on.
The shadows are long.
The air's taken a chill.
I put my key in the gate,
hear the familiar clink of the lock,
and smell the musty entranceway.

Deep in the house of seed
an apple rolls across the floor,
a chant begins and suffers not the sea
but amplifies and feeds
the fleeting tree of we
with birdsong rising from the strand,
a scant release, but full enough for she
who hangs her appling life upon
the seed-wrung, sea-stung breeze.

A dry well is nothing more than a hole in the earth full of strata and bats. Someone put the hole there with their hands and tools. Maybe they had a good long drink. Maybe not. And there it sits, if a hole can sit, sprouting roots and worms and beetles and darkness. What good is it? Well, it's good as a farm for roots and worms and beetles and darkness. It's a darkness farm, squishing out that lovely stuff with every passing day, and specially at night. But rarely does anyone come by to scoop it up. Is it therefore still a farm? Of course! There are many farms that don't get used.

I Daphne May

I'd have my mind the breeze,
My body wood. Fail,
Agility that restricts my
Knowing the moon without thought,
Let me be still free.
I'd have sap my senses,
Fluttering leaves my heart for the air.

COMPOSED ON MOUNT MAJOR, MAY 7, 1982

I am the gentle sloping gray of hillsides
budding yet ungreen, unfolding skyward,
streaked with evergreen and hinting gold
and reddish sprigs unsprung, reclining gray:
I am May smoothing hills to earth
to brooks and rushing rocky currents spilling
into the dark into the cold dark lake,
surface sheening, deep and still, Mother.
I am the rock of Major, grey patched white,
the pine and brambles groping on the ascent,
the hawk in treetops jutting from the slope,
the insects buzzing at the windswept crown:
I found a cliff and pissed into the world,
my member dangling lightly in the breeze.

MEADOW REVERY

I've spoken of pissing off cliffs,
of crouching in caves,
and shorn-legged fords across freezing rapids,
leaping into world with unbridled grin,
but here in this meadow, vast and undulant,
high in the Klamath Hills, safe from sin and sanctimony,
vast with grasses, green and ochre, purple-brown,
edged by Ponderosa, ancient apple, Douglas fir,
white pine, wild cherry, cedar and a hundred more,
here in the middle of life, perhaps past,
sitting in shade of an old black oak,
calm amidst breeze and deep pine scent
in the heat of a late May day,
dense with birdcall, soaked in sky,
abounding flies and ferns at my feet,
I greet world again, and pause, greet and pause again,
city-struck and moon-strung I drift here,
but not quite with the grass, need a month, a year
to soak and shine and twine the lichen once again to
   nerve and vein,
to soak, to breathe, and greet again,
to let that lone hawk tearing from the trees rip me away.

Lying in dark in Bklyn

    & I

hear voices approach the bldg

    & I

        make the city melt away

            they've come in from the woods

               through the estate

                  garden

                    late night dew

                       one late cricket

                         no light for miles

                    up the walk

                     & their laughing

                        echoes on old stone

           breeze comes in from the fields

                  scent of hay

                & I'm pretty sure

                  in the morning

                  I'll throw the curtains wide

ACKNOWLEDGMENTS

Some of these pieces have been previously published in the journals *Prosodia*, *Full of Crow*, *Correspondence*, *Pedestrian*, *Out of Our*, *Pom-Pom*, *Hanging Loose*, *Brooklyn Review*, *Poetry San Francisco*, *nycBigCityLit*, and *Texture*; and in the anthologies *The Careless Embrace of the Boneshaker* and *It's Animal But Merciful* (great weather for MEDIA), *hell strung and crooked* and *you say. say.*, Unhook Press, *Practising Angels*, *The Brownstone Poets Anthology*, and *Austin International Poetry Festival Anthology*. "Composed on Mount Major" appeared in the chapbook *Poetry is a Form of Light*.

THANK YOUS

Thanks to everyone who saw fit to publish some of these pieces in journals and zines: Jane Ormerod, David Lawton, Thomas Fucaloro, George Wallace, Paul Corman-Roberts, E. Lynn Alexander, Linda Lerner, Bob Hershon, Thom Woodruff, Susan Landers, Sarah Gray, Steven Page, Tricia Roush-Peyronnet, Stacey Bernstein, David Fodel, and Michael Mayo, and with a big-hearted RIP, J deSalvo, Brant Lyon, and Herman Berlandt. May you all breathe clarity.

Richard Loranger is a multi-genre writer, performer, musician, and visual artist who has been working around the United States for over forty years. They have lived in many parts of the country, including New York, Austin, Boulder, Ann Arbor, Chicago, and San Francisco, and currently live and work in Oakland, CA. They are the author of *Mammal*, *Unit of Agency*, *Be A Bough Tit*, *Sudden Windows*, *Poems for Teeth*, *The Orange Book*, and ten chapbooks, and have writing in over 100 magazines and journals. You can find more about their work and scandals at www.richardloranger.com. Their email is hello@richardloranger.com.

*

Tobias Brill is an intuitive artist working with expressive surrealism. He works brain to paper or even cosmos to paper and utilizes automatic drawing techniques, exploring in the moment without premeditated outcomes. Tobias graduated from the University of Hawai'i at Hilo and earned a Masters in Fine Arts from Pratt Institute in Brooklyn, NY. He is currently a Lecturer in Art at Hawai'i Community College. His website is www. tobiasbrill.com and Instagram is tobiasbrill94.

ROOF BOOKS

the best in language since 1976

Recent & Selected Titles

- FOR TRAPPED THINGS by Brian Kim Stefans, 138 pp. $20
- EXCURSIVE by Elizabeth Robinson, 140 pp. $20
- I, BOOMBOX by Robert Glück, 194 pp. $20
- TRUE ACCOUNT OF TALKING TO THE 7 IN SUNNYSIDE
  by Paolo Javier, 192 pp. $20
- THE NIGHT BEFORE THE DAY ON WHICH
  by Jean Day, 118 pp. $20
- MINE ECLOGUE by Jacob Kahn, 104 pp. $20
- SCISSORWORK by Uche Nduka, 150 pp. $20
- THIEF OF HEARTS by Maxwell Owen Clark, 116 pp. $20
- DOG DAY ECONOMY by Ted Rees, 138 pp. $20
- THE NERVE EPISTLE by Sarah Riggs, 110 pp. $20
- QUANUNDRUM: [i will be your many angled thing]
  by Edwin Torres, 128 pp. $20
- FETAL POSITION by Holly Melgard, 110 pp. $20
- DEATH & DISASTER SERIES by Lonely Christopher, 192 pp. $20
- THE COMBUSTION CYCLE by Will Alexander, 614 pp. $25
- URBAN POETRY FROM CHINA editors Huang Fan and
  James Sherry, translation editor Daniel Tay, 412 pp. $25
- BIONIC COMMUNALITY by Brenda Iijima, 150 pp. $20
- QUEENZENGLISH.MP3: POETRY: POETRY, PHILOSOPHY,
  PERFORMATIVITY, Edited by Kyoo Lee, 176 pp. $20
- UNSOLVED MYSTERIES by Marie Buck, 96 pp. $18.95

Roof Books are distributed by
SMALL PRESS DISTRIBUTION
1341 Seventh Street • Berkeley, CA. 94710-1403.
spdbooks.org

Roof Books are published by **Segue Foundation**
300 Bowery #2 • New York, NY 10012
seguefoundation.com